Women's Bags

Beautiful and Easy Purse and Bag Patterns to Sew

Copyright © 2021

All rights reserved.

DEDICATION

The author and publisher have provided this e-book to you for your personal use only. You may not make this e-book publicly available in any way. Copyright infringement is against the law. If you believe the copy of this e-book you are reading infringes on the author's copyright, please notify the publisher at: https://us.macmillan.com/piracy

Contents

Easy Felt Tote Bag 1

Flying Geese Patchwork Cinch Sack 8

Jumbo Tote With Striped Pockets 12

Little Girl's Patchwork Purse 21

Reusable Grocery Bag 27

Beach Bag With Rope Handles 32

Mini Quilted Suitcase 40

Envelope-Style Clutch Purse 43

Insulated Lunch Bag 48

Easy Felt Tote Bag

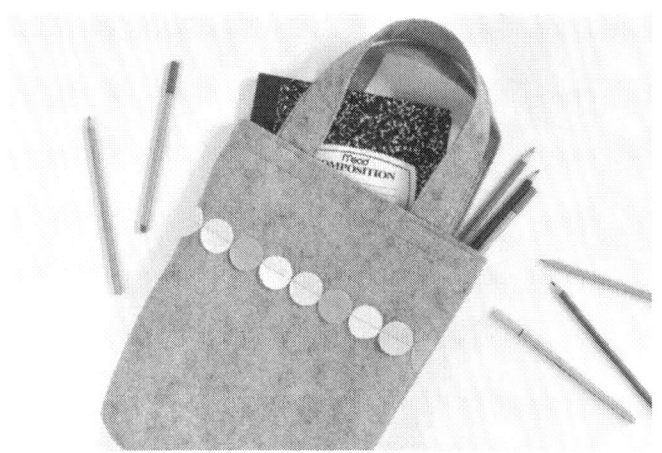

1. Tote Bag Supplies and Cutting Guide

Supplies and Tools

- 1/2 yard of wool blend felt (avoid acrylic craft felt, as it stretches easily)
- Items for decorating, such as extra felt, buttons, embroidery floss, or ribbon
- Craft glue (optional—you'll only need this if you want to glue decorations)
- Thread
- Sewing machine

- Rotary cutter
- Cutting mat
- Ruler
- Straight pins
- Scissors
- Pen

Note: If you don't have a rotary cutter and cutting mat, or if you want to make this safer for young children to make with little assistance, you can carefully use a pair of scissors.

Cutting Guide

Start by cutting the felt for your tote bag. You will need 3 pieces:

- Cut one piece that is 12 inches by 30 inches
- Cut two pieces that each measure 4 inches by 18 inches

All of these sizes are approximate. In fact, once you get the hang of making these easy tote bags, you may want to adjust the size to suit your needs!

The easiest way to cut out these pieces is to fold your 18-inch by 36-inch piece of fabric or felt in half so it is 18 inches by 18 inches. Lay it on your cutting mat and cut a 12-inch by 36-inch piece. Trim it down to 12 inches by 30 inches. Next, cut a 4-inch strip and cut it in half to make two 4-inch by 18-inch pieces.

2. Sew Decorations on the Felt Before Assembling the Bag

There are many ways to decorate a tote bag like this. If you want to attach elements with glue, you should do that at the end of the project. However, if you want to sew decorations on or embellish your bag with embroidery, it's easier to do that before you sew it all together.

The sample bag features a line of felt circles, held in place with a single line of stitching.

You can add any kinds of sewn decorations that you like. Stitch buttons on the felt, embroider a name or fun design (use tissue paper to mark the pattern), or add some felt or fabric applique.

3. Sew the Sides of the Tote Bag

To sew the sides of your tote bag, fold the 12-inch by 30-inch piece of felt in half with the right sides together. Pin and sew each side, using a 1/4-inch seam allowance.

4. Mark the Tote Bag Bottom

To make a "boxed" bottom that will sit flat, start by folding one bottom corner so the side seam lines up with the bottom folded edge. Lay it flat on your work surface as shown.

Use a ruler (a clear ruler is helpful!) and measure up 1 1/2 inches from the point of the fabric. Draw a line perpendicular to the seam. The line should measure 3 inches long with 1 1/2 inches of fabric on either side of the seam.

Repeat on the other side of the tote bag.

5. Sew and Trim the Tote Bag Bottom

Sew along each marked corner line. Lock stitch at the beginning and end of the sewing.

Trim the threads and then cut off the points, leaving about 1/4 inch of fabric.

Turn the tote bag right side out.

6. Make the Tote Bag Handles

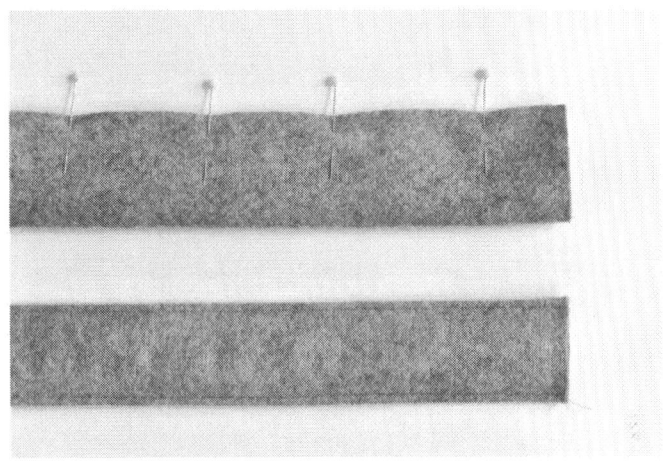

To make the tote bag handles, fold each 4-inch by 18-inch piece of felt in half and pin the long edge. Sew each piece with a 1/4-inch seam allowance.

Turn the handles right side out. One way to do this is by attaching a safety pin to one open end and feeding it through the tube until it comes out the other end.

Once your tote bag handles are right side out, topstitch up each long side, about 1/8 inch from each edge.

7. Attach the Handles to the Tote Bag

At the top edge of the tote bag, measure in 2 inches from each seam and make a small mark. Line up the outside edge of one end of the first handle with a marking.

Hold the end of the handle so it lines up with the top edge of the tote bag and pin in place. Pin the other end of the handle in place next to the other marking using this same method. Make sure that the handle isn't twisted.

Repeat this on the other side of the tote bag for the other handle.

Sew around the top edge of the bag with a 1/2-inch seam allowance to secure the handles in place.

8. Fold and Pin the Top of the Tote Bag

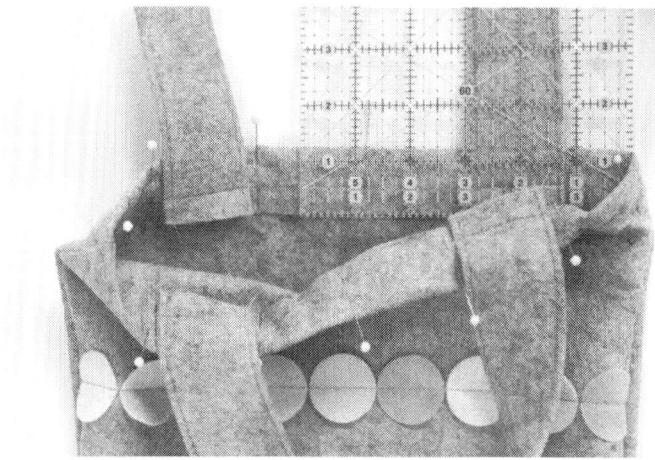

To finish your tote bag, fold about 1 1/4 inch of the top edge of the bag into the tote bag. The handles should now be up and away from the bag. Pin around the top of the bag.

9. Sew the Top of the Tote Bag

Sew around the top edge of the tote bag to hold the fold and the handle ends in place. First, sew about 1/4 inch from the inside edge of the felt, and then sew about 1/4 inch down from the folded top edge.

Trim the threads and your easy tote bag is ready to go. Now you can add other decorations or start using it right away!

Flying Geese Patchwork Cinch Sack

Materials to make a Flying Geese Bucket Bag:

Assortment of 11 fat quarters, 10 solids and 1 print for geese

3/4 yard of wide canvas or other heavyweight cloth for lining

10 Dritz 0.44" Metal Grommets

2 1/2 yards of twisted cotton rope

Round 10 1/2 inch plate

Flying Geese Paper Piece Template

To start, cut 2 sets of 2 1/2" x 15 1/2" strips from each solid fat quarter, except for the piece that will be your bottom stripe. For the bottom stripe, cut 2 6 1/2" strips and 2 9 1/2" strips.

Next, grab your 10 1/2" plate and trace it on your lining fabric like so…

Cut out the circles and set aside. Next up, cut 4 2 1/4" x 2 2 1/2" squares from the canvas and set aside. Next, cut a 20 1/2" x 34 1/2" piece of canvas.

Make your flying geese. There are so many ways to make flying geese. When I only have a few to make for a project I paper piece them. Since they are the main focal point of this bag, you want to be sure they are precise. You'll find a paper piecing template for the geese in this pattern. (If you have never paper pieced, check out this great tutorial by Jennifer Mathis of Ellison Lane.)

For your geese, use the print you have chosen for your geese's center and use scraps from the fat quart solids for the background. You will make ten of these, one for each solid color you have chosen.

Once you have removed your paper from the geese, sew each one in the middle of your two 15 1/2" long strips (for the bottom strip of your bag, attach the 9 1/2" long strip and set aside). Be sure to match the background color of the geese to the strip color (or go super scrappy and mix them up!).

Sew your strips together (all but the bottom stripe) using a 1/4" seam. Pin your seams so they match up. I used Patchwork Foot #97D with seam guide for this part. Points always come out perfectly!

Your piece should measure 18 1/2" x 34 1/2".

Remember those 4 2 1/4" x 2 2 1/2" canvas pieces? Grab those guys and sew together three of the sides with a 1/4" seam allowance to make two tabs, leaving one of the 2 1/4" sides open. Trim off some of the seam allowance and flip them. Press your seams.

Time to grommet! Use the instructions on the box to add grommets to the tabs. I placed mine just over 1/4" from the finished edge, centering it from the top and bottom. This was my first time using grommets and it was so easy. It gives such a polished look to the bag.

Grab your last strips (your bottom stripe). Pin the 6 1/2" strips to either side of the goose strip, placing the grommet tab in the center.

Here is the layout for the bottom stripe of the bag. From left to right, the order should be 6 1/2" strip, tab, 9 1/2" strip, goose, 9 1/2" strip, tab, 6 1/2" strip

Lower your stitch length to 1.20mm. Sew with a 1/4" seam allowance. I went back and forth a few times to give it strength.

Add your last strip to the 18 1/2" x 34 1/2" piece (be sure when you are adding the strip with the tabs that you are careful not to catch the tabs in your seam).

Your piece should now measure 20 1/2" x 34 1/2". Right sides together, sew up the 20 1/2" side of the panel. Pin your seams so they match. Use a 1/2" seam allowance, keeping your stitch length at 1.20mm. When you are done, flip it around and press your back seam.

Jumbo Tote With Striped Pockets

Supplies and Tools

1-1/3 yard of 60" wide linen - canvas, denim or another heavy-duty fabric also works

1-1/4 yard of midweight fusible interfacing

1/8 yard each of four colorful cotton fabrics

2/3 yard of lining fabric - quilting cotton or linen to match the outside

3 2/3 yards of 1-1/2" wide cotton webbing

Thread

Optional: 3 2/3 yards of ribbon to embellish the straps

Optional: 4" by 14-1/2" piece of lightweight chipboard, corrugated plastic or similar sturdy material for the base of the bag

Rotary cutter, ruler, and cutting mat

Iron and ironing board

Pins

Sewing machine

Scissors

Cutting Guide

Main Fabric (linen):

Cut one 40" by 20"

Cut two 20" by 9.5"

Interfacing:

Cut one 40" by 20" (alternately, you can iron this to the linen before you cut the 40" by 20" piece)

Pocket Fabrics (colorful cotton):

Cut two 20" by 2.75" from each of four fabrics

Lining Fabric (quilting cotton or linen):

Cut one 39" by 20"

Instructions

Outside Pockets

Note: During the construction of this bag, it is important to remain accurate with seam allowances and placement measurements so that the outside pocket sections line up properly as the bag comes together. As long as you are accurate and consistent, the outside pockets will appear to be one continuous strip around the bag.

Sew four of the strips of fabric to make a striped panel. Use 1/4" seam allowances. Repeat with the other four strips. Press the seam allowances toward the darker fabric.

Sew the Pocket Pieces

Pin the pocket backing to the front of the striped panel and, using a 1/4" seam allowance, sew the fabrics together along the 20" edges. Repeat for the second set of pieces.

Press the seams to set them.

Turn the joined fabric sections right side out and press well, making sure that the seams are open and at the very edges of the sections.

Topstitch the Striped Pocket Pieces

Topstitch 1/8" from the top edge of the pocket, then topstitch 1/8" on each side of the stripe seams. You may want to pin the layers together while sewing to prevent the layers from shifting.

Leave the bottom edge plain and without topstitching.

Place and Sew the Outside Pockets

If you didn't attach the interfacing to the main piece of the bag before cutting, do that now.

Lay the main part of the bag flat with the interfacing side down. If there are any wrinkles press the piece before proceeding.

Measure and mark 5 1/2" from each 20" end of the strip of fabric. Place the top-stitched edge of each pocket along the markings and pin the pocket sections in place.

Double check your measurements to be sure the pockets are straight and that they line up when you fold the body of the bag in half.

Sew the bottom each pocket section to the main part of the bag piece, stitching 1/8" from the edge so it matches the other topstitching.

Baste the side edges of the pockets to the main part of the bag, sewing about 1/8" from the edge. You can also sew around the entire main bag piece to finish prevent fraying.

Fold the bag in half and gently press the center fold line. The pressed line will be used for lining up pieces but is not a part of the finished bag.

Attach the Handles

Fold the length of the webbing in half and mark the halfway point.

Measure 5" inches in from each long edge of the bag.

Place the halfway mark on the strap on the center fold line with the edge of the strap on the 5" markings.

Without twisting the cotton webbing, bring the two ends of the strap to the center fold line on the opposite side of the bag, again on the 5" markings. You can either butt the ends of the strap together or overlap them by about 1".

Pin the strap in place, making sure it remains straight.

Sew along the edge of the straps, stopping and pivoting 2 1/2" from each end. At the ends, you may want to backstitch across the strap for added strength.

Repeat on the remaining strap.

Sew the Outside of the Bag

Fold the right sides of the bag together matching the pockets at the side edges.

Pin and sew the side seams using a 1/2" seam allowance. Press the seams, then iron inside the bag to press the seam to one side or the other.

Fold the bag so the side seam is directly over the bottom fold line on the bottom of the bag.

Measure and mark 2" in from the corner. Stitch a perpendicular line across the side seam at the 2" mark, backstitching at both ends of the seam.

Trim off the triangle, leaving a 1/2" seam allowance.

Make the Lining

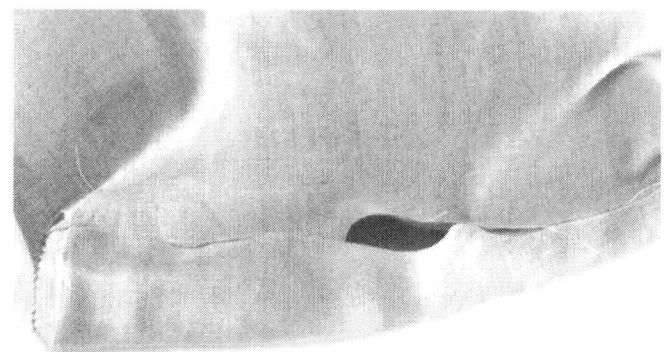

Sew 1/8" around the 20" by 39" lining piece to prevent fraying (or apply a seam finish after assembling the lining).

Fold the 39" edges in half with right sides together. Align the edges and pin the two sides.

Sew the side seams using a 1/2" seam allowance, leaving a gap on one side for turning. Be sure to backstitch on each side of the opening

Sew the squared bottom corners the same way you did for the outside of the bag.

Sew the Lining Into the Bag

With the outside of the bag right side out and the lining inside out, insert the main bag inside the right side of the lining.

Match the side seams and the edges of the lining to the edges of the bag.

Pin and sew the lining and bag together.

Turn and Finish the Tote Bag

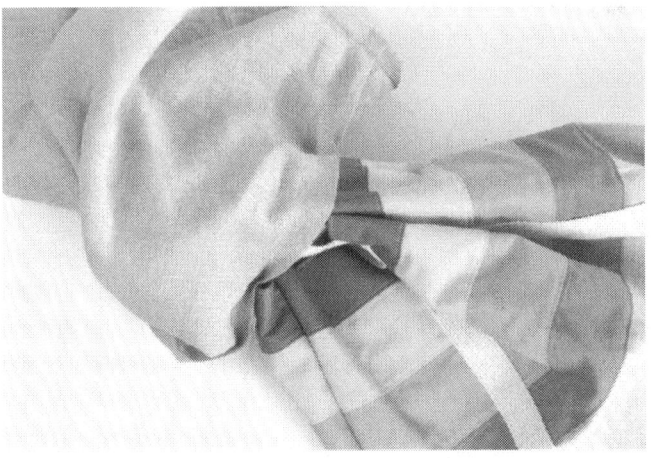

Turn the bag right side out, pulling it through the gap in the lining.

Fold the seam allowance on the gap so it matches the side seam, then sew it closed. You can do this by hand for a more invisible seam or by machine, sewing close to the folded seam allowance.

Push the lining into the bag.

Press the top edge of the bag, then topstitch 1/8" from the top seam.

If you'd like the bottom of the bag to sit flat, place a 4" by 14 1/2" piece of chipboard or corrugated plastic inside of the bag.

Little Girl's Patchwork Purse

Littlest Girl: approx. 7" wide x 5 1/4" tall

Fabric:

30 – 2.5" squares for patchwork

1- 10 1/2" x 12" piece for lining

1- 2 1/2" x 13" piece for strap

1- 25" x 2 1/2" piece for binding

Fusible Interfacing:

1- 2 1/4" x 13" for strap

Flannel:

2- 1" x 12" for strap

Fusible Fleece:

1- 10 1/2" x 12 1/2" for body of bag

Little Girl: approx. 9" wide x 6 1/2" tall

Fabric:

30 – 3" squares for patchwork

1- 13" x 15" piece for lining

1- 3" x 14" piece for strap

1- 3o" x 3" piece for binding

Fusible Interfacing:

1 – 2 3/4" x 14 for strap

Flannel:

2- 1" x 14" for strap

Fusible Fleece:

1- 13" x 15 1/2" for body of bag

Instructions

Choosing the fabric is my favorite part. You will have two squares of each print, this will make the front and back of the purse look the same. This is not necessary, it's the way I made mine.

Sew the patchwork squares five across by three down using 1/4" seam allowances. Make two panels, these will be the front and the back of purse.

Sew the two panels together to create one piece. Make sure the squares are opposing each other at the opposite ends so they will be correct. Fuse the fusible fleece to the back of the panel. (Follow the directions on the product you are using.) Quilt the squares 1/4" on either side of the seams to create a patchwork piece.

Sew the side seams with right sides together using a 3/8" seam allowance. Pin in place to make sure your squares line up at the seams.

Press the side seams open and fold the sides to create a point, measure 1 1/4" from the point, draw a line with a pencil or pen, then sew across this line, cut excess off leaving a 1/4" seam allowance. This will make a box at the bottom of purse. For the larger size purse draw a line 1 1/2" from the point and sew a seam then cut leaving a

1/4" seam allowance.

Trim off the excess and leave 1/4" seam.

Turn the purse right side out. Place a pin in the middle of the purse front and back for the pleat.

Take the seam from the adjoining squares and pin at the middle where the other pin is. This will make the pleat. Do this for both the front and back.

Sew along the top edge to hold the pleat in place. Sew the lining piece the same as you did for the outer purse, side seams, and corners. Place the lining inside the bag wrong sides together. Make the pleat using the outside of the purse for the guide, pin in place. Stitch along the top edge of the purse to hold them together.

Fold the binding piece in half lengthwise and press. (top strip)

Fuse the interfacing to the wrong side of the strap piece. (bottom strip)Sew the strap in half lengthwise to create a long tube, press the seam allowance open.

lTurn the strap using a safety-pin or bodkin. Press it flat with the seam running down the middle back. Feed the flannel through the tube with the safety-pin or bodkin. Stitch along the long edge of the strap 1/8" and 1/4" to finish it.

Pin the strap along the side seams, making sure to place the seam of the strap downward with the seam of the lining. After sewing it in place trim excess flannel.

Attach the binding to the top of the purse, leaving tails open at the beginning and end of the binding piece. Sew the ends into a complete circle. Now sew the unsewn portion of binding onto the top of the bag.

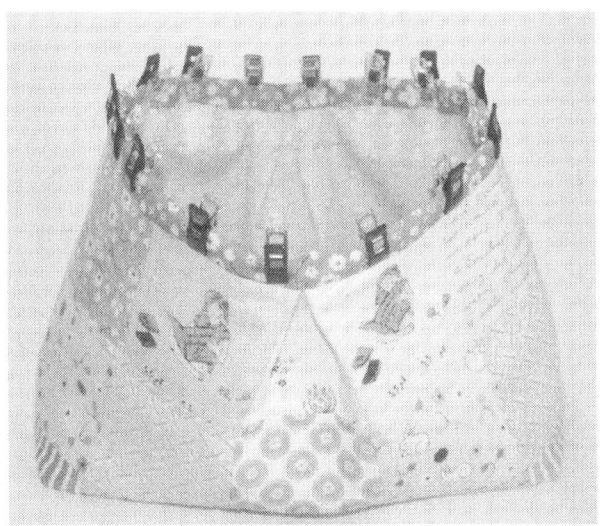

After the binding is sewn all the way around the top of the purse fold it over to the inside of the purse and stitch it down.

Sewing-strap-to-side-15Now pull the strap up and sew a stitching line to secure the strap in place.

Reusable Grocery Bag

Equipment / Tools

Rotary cutter, ruler, and cutting mat

Pins

Sewing machine

Iron

Materials

3/4 yard 45"-wide durable fabric such as canvas or denim

3/4 yard 45"-wide cotton fabric for the lining

1 1/3 yards 1"-wide webbing

Instructions

1. Gather Materials

Strong utility fabrics, such as canvas or denim, work best for a grocery tote, but that doesn't mean they have to be boring. Look for bold prints -online or from a variety of fabric stores- so you have lots of choices.

Note: Always preshrink the fabric so it doesn't shrink the first time you need to wash the bag.

You can use a regular ruler, any marking tool, and scissors, but it's faster and easier to use a rotary cutter with a special ruler and mat designed to work together.

Reusable Grocery Bag Materials

2. Cutting and Marking

Make the following cuts from the corresponding material:

1 rectangle 37" x 14" of both the outer and lining fabrics for the body

2 rectangles 15" x 8" of both the outer and lining fabrics for the sides

2 pieces of webbing 24"-long for the straps

Fold in half and crease to mark the centers of both 37" edges on the body of the bag and the centers of one 8" edge on each side piece.

3. Sew the Body/Sides

Pin one exterior side piece to one exterior bag piece right sides together, matching the center markings on both. Using a 3/8" seam allowance and backstitching at beginning and end, sew down one side, pivot at the bottom corner, sew across the base, pivot, and sew up to the top of the bag. Repeat on the other side of the bag. For extra strength, backstitch the bottom corners. Trim the corners to reduce bulk.

Repeat the same process to sew the lining together, this time using a 1/2" seam allowance.

4. Finish the Seam Allowances

If needed, apply a seam finish to the outer bag piece to prevent the raw edges from fraying. If you see any fabric fraying as you work, take the time to complete this step because it will help your bag last longer.

Trimming with pinking shears is a fast and easy way to do this. You could also zig-zag the edges, use a serger, or apply a seam sealant. Press the seams.

5. Attach the Straps

Measure in 3" from the side seams along the top edge of one wide side of the bag body. Pin one piece of webbing at the marks, leaving an inch of the webbing extending above the top of the bag. Sew across each end of the straps three or four times 1/4" from the edge of the fabric. This acts as basting, but it also helps keep the straps secure. Repeat on the opposite side.

6. Attach the Lining

With the outer bag turned wrong side out and the lining turned right side out, nest the lining inside the outer bag. Pin around the upper edge. Using a 3/8" seam allowance, sew the outer bag and lining together, leaving a 5" opening on one side.

Finish the top seam as you did the others, making sure not to close the opening. Turn the bag right side out through the opening.

7. Top Stitch to Finish

Push the lining into the bag and press the top seam, folding the seam allowances of the opening inside, even with the sewn edge. Topstitch around the top of the bag 1/8" from the seam, closing the opening, and again 5/8" from the seam. Sew a box with an X through each strap end to securely hold the straps in place.

Take your new bag to the market on your next shopping trip and load it up with groceries!

Beach Bag With Rope Handles

SUPPLIES:

This post may include affiliate links

3/4 yard of fabric for bag center

3/4 yards of fabric for bag side panels

1 yard of fabric for lining

1 Fat Quarter for Pocket

2 yards 20" wide fusible flex foam

2 yards 20" wide Shape Flex Interfacing

4 One inch curtain grommets

3 yards of 1/2 cotton rope – I purchased my rope HERE.

3 yards of pom pom trim

Other:

Masking tape

Fabric Safe marking pens

CUTTING DIRECTIONS:

From Bag Center Fabric:

2 pieces each 10" x 20"

From Bag Side Fabric:

4 pieces each 8" x 20"

From Pocket Fabric:

1 piece 8" x 10"

From Shape Flex Interfacing:

2 pieces each 10" x 20"

4 pieces each 8" x 20"

Bag Lining Fabric is cut at a later point.

CONSTRUCTION STEPS:

Iron Shape flex interfacing onto the wrong side of the bag center and bag side pieces. Refer to the directions on the package for pressing instructions.

On two of the bag side pieces cut a 3" x 3" square from the bottom right corner.

On the other two bag side pieces cut a 3" x 3" square from the bottom left corner.

Pair one bag side piece cut from the right corner with one bag side piece cut from the left corner. Repeat.

Learn how to sew a cute oversized pool bag with this Oversized Beach Bag Sewing Pattern - so roomy and such a simple free pattern!

Pin Pom Pom trim to the long side of the bag side piece (on the side without the square-cut out). The edge of the Pom Pom trim should be flush with the raw edge of the fabric.

Using a zig-zag stitch attach pom pom trim to the bag side piece. Stop the pom pom trim 3" from the bottom of the piece.

Repeat for other 3 bag side pieces.

TO CREATE THE BAG OUTSIDE FRONT PIECE:

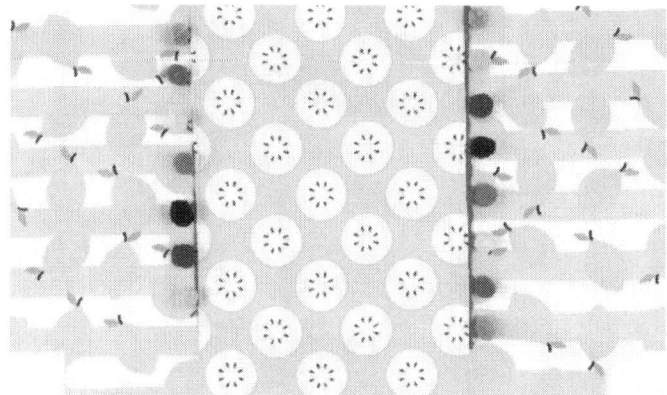

Learn how to sew a cute oversized pool bag with this Oversized Beach Bag Sewing Pattern - so roomy and such a simple free pattern!

Learn how to sew a cute oversized pool bag with this Oversized Beach Bag Sewing Pattern - so roomy and such a simple free pattern!

Pin two bag side pieces right sides facing to the bag front piece along the long edge. The cut-out corner will be on the outside (this is why you need a right and a left bag side pieces).

Stitch with a 5/8" seam allowance.

Press seam towards the bag center pieces. Top stitch along the seam between the bag center and bag side pieces.

Repeat with other bag side/ bag center pieces to create the bag outside back piece.

Set aside

CONSTRUCT THE POCKET:

Fold the bag pocket piece in half right sides facing. Stitch around 3 sides of the pocket leaving 2" -3" opening on one side of the pocket so you can turn it right side out.

Clip corners, turn right side out and press. Top stitch one of the long sides – this will be the top of your pocket.

CUT AND CONSTRUCT THE BAG LINING:

Using one of your bag outside pieces as a guide, cut 2 bag lining pieces and 2 pieces from fusible flex foam.

Trim 1/2" off the top of each piece of flex foam.

Press the fusible flex foam onto the wrong side of the bag lining pieces. You should have 1/2" of fabric hanging over the edge of the flex foam at the top.

Learn how to sew a cute oversized pool bag with this Oversized Beach Bag Sewing Pattern - so roomy and such a simple free pattern!

Pin the pocket to one of the bag lining pieces in the center of the lining and a few inches down from the top edge of the lining.

Stitch around 3 sides of the pocket to secure. Make sure you backstitch.

ASSEMBLE THE BAG:

Pin the two bag outside pieces together, right sides facing. Stitch the center and bottom seams using a 1/2" seam allowance.

Press seams open.

Pinch one of the bottom corners of the bag so that the side and bottom seams are on top of each other and stitch using a 1/2" seam allowance. Repeat for other bottom corner.

Stitch the bag lining pieces together just as you did for the bag outside pieces. Trim the seam allowances down to 1/4" to reduce bulk.

Turn bag lining piece so that the right side of the fabric is facing out.

Slip the bag lining piece into the bag outside piece, right sides facing. Make sure that you match the bag centers and side seams. Pin well.

Stitch along the top edge of the bag 1/2" down from the raw edge of the fabric. You will be stitching right up to the edge of the flex foam interfacing.

Leave a 9" opening on one side of the bag so that you can turn the bag right side out.

Turn bag right side out. Press top seam well, making sure to catch the opening that you used to turn the bag right side out and press.

Top stitch along the top of the bag.

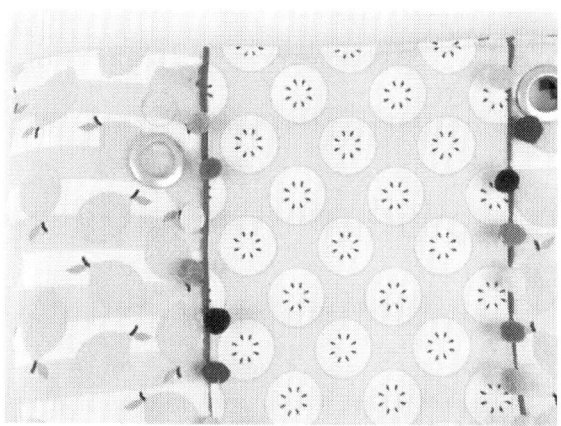

FINISHING:

Following the directions on the package of grommets attach 2 grommets to each side of the bag 1" down from the top edge of the bag and just over from the seam between the bag center and bag side pieces.

Cut your rope to your desired length. Before you cut wrap a piece of masking tape around the end of the rope so it does not unravel while you are working with it. I cut my rope pieces to 40" long.

Learn how to sew a cute oversized pool bag with this Oversized Beach Bag Sewing Pattern - so roomy and such a simple free pattern!

Feed rope through the hole in the grommet and tie a knot. After you have the rope in the location that you want, remove the masking tape from the end of the rope and allow it to fray up to the knot.

Give the bag a good pressing and you're done!

Mini Quilted Suitcase

You'll need

- Plain Canvas Tote
- 2 Coordinating fabrics for bow and border
- Matching ribbon

Canvas totes are all different sizes so you'll want to take into consideration how big your tote is when you're cutting out your fabrics.

Measure out a fabric panel for the bottom of the tote – 4" tall and 1" wider than your tote. Press the top and bottom of your fabric under 1/2".

Fold the two short sides in 1/2" as well. Sew in place at the bottom of the tote, making sure you don't catch any of the tote or handles while you sew.

Cut out two pieces of coordinating fabric that are 7" x 22". Cut two ends of the fabric at a diagonal, opposite of each other. Hem the top and bottom and the diagonal edge of the pieces.

Place the fabric pieces at each side of the tote. The diagonal edges should angle down for each piece. Turn the raw edges under along the left and right sides of the tote and sew the pieces down along each side. Gather the fabrics in the center and wrap a piece of ribbon around them to form the bow. Sew the ribbon in place.

Sew the ribbon down to the inside of the tote to hold it in place. Tack the tops of the bow pieces about 2" in from each side to keep the bow straight.

Cut two lengths of ribbon 1" longer than each strap. Fold the ends under and sew in place on the front of each strap.

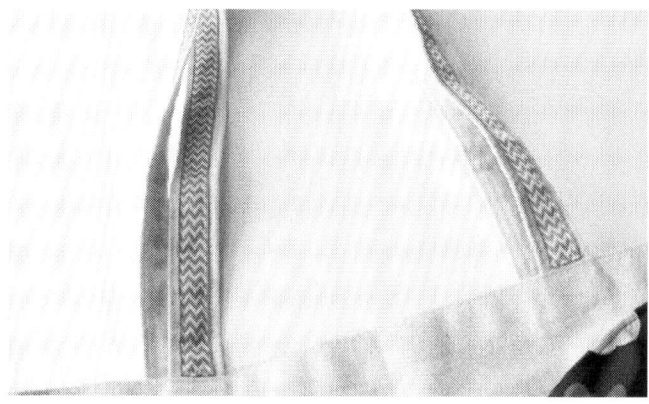

That's it! You have a cute new tote refashion!

You can really change up the style by just changing the fabrics and adding in some lace!

Envelope-Style Clutch Purse

Materials:

1/2 yard fabric (or 1 fat quarter)

1/2 yard lining (or 1 fat quarter)

1/2 yard midweight fusible interfacing

1 button, any size

Envelope Clutch Pattern

Additional supplies:

-needle & thread for closing

–pinking shears(optional)

Notes:

*Use 3/8" seam allowance

*seam allowance included in the pattern

Instructions:

Print pattern piece and tape together. The pages will overlap and fit together like so: (Use the grey lines and boxes to line up the pages.)

Cut it out and cut out 1 each from your main fabric, lining and interfacing.

Fuse interfacing to back of main fabric piece.

Set the main piece (with interfacing on the bottom) with the top flap away from you. The edge you see in this photo is the bottom edge of the clutch.

Fold the sides up at the notch and pin them.

When both are pinned, it will look like this. The piece that is sticking up in the air is the top flap piece.

Sew up the two sides you just pinned.

Repeat with the lining piece, but this time leave a 3-4" opening while sewing one of the sides to the bottom. Backstitch at both ends.

Press the seam allowances up.

Turn the lining right sides out and slip into the main piece. The main piece will still be turned wrong sides out so the right side of the lining will match up to the the right side of the main piece.

Pin all the way around.

When pinning the top flap, pull the lining out and extra 1/8" to 1/4". This is a little trick that will help the lining stay on the inside of your clutch, so it doesn't peek out.

Sew all the edges, then trim the straight edges and trim/clip (or pink) the curved edge.

Find the hole you left in the lining and use that to pull your clutch right sides out.

Press the clutch and turn the lining to the outside.

Sew it up using a slip stitch.

Add a buttonhole. (Tutorial coming tomorrow!) Sew on your button and you're done!

Insulated Lunch Bag

MATERIALS:

1/2 yd Oilcloth fabric

1/2 yd Ripstop nylon fabric

1/2 yd Needlepunched insulated lining

14" Zipper

1 yd 1" Polyester webbing

Coordinating thread

Universal regular point sewing needles

Fabric scissors

Ruler

Binder clips

Sewing machine

materials list for insulated lunch bag

INSTRUCTIONS:

Cut (1) 24" x 14" of: – Oilcloth (exterior) – Nylon rip stop (lining) – Insul bright

Place the Insul Bright along the wrong side of the oilcloth, matching up all edges. If desired, baste stitch around all side seams using a 1/4" seam allowance to help secure.

Align outer edge of zipper, right sides together with side edge of oilcloth. Place rip stop fabric on top, sandwiching the zipper in between. Clip in place along side edge.

Sew using a zipper foot, getting 1/4" away from the zipper teeth.

Open fabric at seam, showing the zipper in the middle. Bring opposite edge of oilcloth to opposite side of zipper, right sides together. Repeat for rip stop, once again sandwiching the zipper in the middle. Clip in place.

Sew using your zipper foot, getting 1/4" away from the zipper teeth.

Place exterior and lining right sides together, with the zipper in the middle. Clip around side edges, leaving a 5" opening for turning in the lining. Sew and trim seam allowance.

Turn bag right side out through opening in lining. Pin opening in lining closed and sew.

With bag wrong side out, flatten corner edges into triangles, centering the side seam. Clip triangle edges to hold in place. Sew a straight line across bottom of triangle. Repeat for other side. Trim seam allowance and turn bag right side out.

Cut (2) 15" pieces of webbing.

Fold bottom edge of webbing 1/2" towards wrong side.

Find center of purse, and measure out 3" on both sides. Pin folded edge of webbing 2" from top on either side. Repeat for opposite side of bag. Sew around webbing bottom to secure.

Manufactured by Amazon.ca
Bolton, ON